Teaching Reading

Richard R. Day

English
Language
Teacher
Development
Series

Thomas S. C. Farrell,
Series Editor

Typeset in Janson and Frutiger
by Capitol Communications, LLC, Crofton, Maryland USA
and printed by Gasch Printing, LLC, Odenton, Maryland USA

TESOL International Association
1925 Ballenger Avenue
Alexandria, Virginia 22314 USA
Tel 703-836-0774 • Fax 703-836-7864

Publishing Manager: Carol Edwards
Cover Design: Tomiko Breland
Copyeditor: Jean House

TESOL Book Publications Committee
John I. Liontas, Chair

Maureen S. Andrade	Joe McVeigh
Jennifer Lebedev	Gail Schafers
Robyn L. Brinks Lockwood	Lynn Zimmerman

Project overview: John I. Liontas and Robyn L. Brinks Lockwood
Reviewer: Soonyoung Hwang An

ISBN 9781931185998

Contents

About the Author

Dr. Richard R. Day is Professor of Second Language Studies, University of Hawaii. His professional interests include second language reading and materials design and development. Dr. Day's most recent publication is *New Ways in Teaching Reading, revised*, a collection of 120 activities for teaching second language reading (2012, TESOL International).

Series Editor's Preface

The English Language Teacher Development (ELTD) Series is a set of short resource books for ESL/EFL teachers that are written in a jargon-free and accessible manner for all types English language teachers (native and nonnative speakers of English, experienced and novice teachers). The ELTD Series is designed to offer teachers a theory-to-practice approach to English language teaching, and each book offers a wide variety of practical teaching approaches and methods for the topic at hand. Each book also offers opportunities for reflections that allow teachers to interact with the materials presented. The books can be used in preservice settings or in-service courses and by individuals who are looking for ways to refresh their practice.

Richard Day's book *Teaching Reading* explores different approaches to teaching reading in English language classrooms. As the author notes in his conclusion, the overarching goal of this book is to engage teachers in reflection on how reading may be taught to ESOL learners. This comprehensive overview of the reading process and how to teach reading provides an easy-to-follow guide that language teachers will find very practical for their own contexts. Topics covered include the nature of reading, reading strategies, reading fluency, reading comprehension, and the reading lesson. *Teaching Reading* is a valuable addition to the literature in our profession.

I am very grateful to the authors who contributed to the ELTD Series for sharing their knowledge and expertise with other TESOL professionals because they have done so willingly and without any compensation to make these short books affordable to language teachers throughout the world. It was truly an honor for me to work with each of these authors as they selflessly gave up their valuable time for the advancement of TESOL.

Thomas S. C. Farrell

1

What Is Reading?

One way to introduce the nature of reading is to directly engage the reader (you) and to ask you to think about what you are doing, mentally, as you read this sentence. So stop reading, look away from the page, and think about the act of reading and what you did when you read the first sentence.

REFLECTIVE BREAK

Complete this sentence:

- Reading is _____.

Your answer probably had something to do with comprehension, meaning, or understanding. This is the most common way that people think of reading. This view of reading as comprehension is generally thought of as a cognitive or mental view of reading—of what takes place in the brain. A useful cognitive definition is

> *Reading is a number of interactive processes between
> the reader and the text, in which readers use their
> knowledge to build, to create, and to construct meaning.*

This chapter covers some of the keywords in this simple but helpful definition. The first keyword is *interactive*. This keyword refers to two different conceptions: (1) the interaction that occurs between the reader and the text, whereby the reader constructs meaning based partly on the knowledge drawn from the text and partly from the existing knowledge that the reader has; and (2) the interactivity occurring simultaneously among the many component skills that results in comprehension. As Grabe (1991) notes, the interactive reading processes involve "both an array of low-level rapid, automatic identification skills and an array of higher-level comprehension/interpretation skills" (p. 383).

Another keyword is *processes*. A number of processes are at work when people read. Grabe (2009) identifies "lower-level processes, including word recognition, syntactic parsing and meaning encoding as propositions" and "higher-level processing, including text-model formation (what the text is about), situation-model building (how we decide to interpret the text), inferencing, executive-control processing (how we direct our attention), and strategic processing" (p. 21).

Also critical is *knowledge*. Actually, perhaps *knowledges* would be more accurate. This includes knowledge of the language (e.g., the writing system, grammar, vocabulary), knowledge of the topic of the text, knowledge of the author, knowledge of the genre (e.g., editorial in a newspaper, a romance novel), and knowledge of the world, including experiences, values, and beliefs. People use all of these knowledges to build, to create, and to construct meaning. Readers all have different knowledge.

REFLECTIVE BREAK

- Two people read the same book. Will they construct the same meaning?

- Why or why not?

The best answer is, *Probably not because they have different knowledges.* They could have similar knowledges, so perhaps their meanings could be similar, but they would probably not construct identical meanings.

REFLECTIVE BREAK

Now reflect on your teaching:

- If you teach ESOL reading, do you let your students read?

- Do you allow them to create or construct their own meaning?

- Or do you insist on your meaning?

There are other dimensions of reading. For example, reading can be seen as a *cultural* event. All reading takes place in a given culture; culture shapes what, how, where, and when people read. Indeed, culture even determines whether people engage in reading. Some cultures are what may be called *nonreading* cultures. In a nonreading culture, in general, people tend not to read. For example, in a nonreading culture, people generally are not seen reading on buses or trains. By contrast, in a reading culture, people read at every opportunity.

Still another view of reading is *affective*. This affective dimension sees reading as *enjoyment*, *pleasure*, *excitement*, even *magic*. Without leaving their chairs, readers can visit a different city, a different country, a new and strange world. They can leap ahead in time and space or visit the distant past. Readers experiencing this magical dimension of reading may lose track of time and space. They forget what time it is and where they are. Psychologists call this a *flow experience*.

REFLECTIVE BREAK

Reflect on flow and your reading in both your first language (L1) and a second language (L2):

- When you read in your L1, do you have flow experiences?

- When you read in a L2, do you have flow experiences?

- Do your students have flow when reading in English?

- How might you create the conditions for flow when your students read English?

Conclusion

This chapter examined the nature of reading and looked at three dimensions of reading: cognitive, cultural, and affective.

> ### REFLECTIVE BREAK
>
> Before moving to Chapter 2, consider these reflection questions:
>
> - What is the most important thing you have learned in this chapter?
>
> - Why is it important?

2

Beliefs About ESOL Reading

This chapter is a questionnaire with two parts. Part A asks about your beliefs about how ESOL students learn to read, and Part B concerns the teaching of ESOL reading. Read each statement, reflect on it, and then mark it according to the scale. Bear in mind that this questionnaire is not a test. Rather, it an instrument to help you reflect on your beliefs about learning and teaching ESOL reading. After you have finished, move to Chapter 3.

A. How important is each statement about learning to read English as a second or foreign language? Use this scale:

Not at all important	Unimportant	Important	Very Important
1	2	3	4

___ 1. Analyzing syntactic structures of texts

___ 2. Reading a great deal

___ 3. Reading material that is interesting

___ 4. Reading material that is easy (within the student's linguistic ability)

___ 5. Reading for enjoyment and pleasure

___ 6. Reading for complete (100%) understanding, including vocabulary

___ 7. Translating texts from English to the student's L1

___ 8. Engaging in pre-reading activities

___ 9. Answering comprehension questions after reading

___10. Reading challenging texts

B. How important is each statement about teaching reading (in English) to speakers of other languages?

Not at all important	Unimportant	Important	Very Important
1	2	3	4

___ 1. Teaching students a variety of strategies (e.g., scanning, finding the main idea)

___ 2. Teaching students to learn to read at a rate (speed) appropriate for their purpose for reading

___ 3. Giving students information about a text before they read it (e.g., telling them something about the topic or the author)

___ 4. Being a role model (i.e., reading English or other L2 texts yourself)

___ 5. Providing opportunities for students to discuss what they have read with each other

___ 6. Allowing students to select their own reading material

___ 7. Having the goal of enjoying reading

___ 8. Making available to students a variety of reading material on a wide range of topics

___ 9. Making sure that the primary activity of a reading lesson is learners' reading

3

How Do People Learn to Read?

This chapter turns to the topic of learning to read. By the end of the chapter, you will understand how people learn to read in either their L1 or their L2.

REFLECTIVE BREAK

To begin, think about how you learned to read in your L1. Then complete the following sentence:

• People learn to read _____.

The only answer is *People learn to read by reading.* There is no other way: The more people read, the better readers they become. Reading is a skill—a learned behavior—so in order to learn to do it, learners must engage in it. This is true whether it is learning to read, to cook, to drive a car, or to play the piano.

Think about this: When the teacher is talking in the reading class, are the students reading? The answer is obviously *no.* The teacher is robbing the students of the opportunity to do the only thing that will help them learn to read, and that is reading. As explained previously, people learn to read by reading. This is true of a first language, a second, third, and so on.

There are, however, differences between L1 and L2 reading developmental processes. The reading developmental processing differences may be classified as linguistic (e.g., grammar, vocabulary), individual (e.g., learners' L1 reading abilities, motivation), and sociocultural.

Because ESOL learners are from widely varying cultures with different languages and educational backgrounds, there is no single template for how reading teachers should modify their instruction. What ESOL reading teachers can do is learn from their experiences. When learners' first language writing systems are radically different from English, teachers might be able to explore what helps such learners and what does not. Talking with other ESOL reading teachers and sharing experiences is also helpful.

Conclusion

This chapter has examined how people learn to read. The next topic concerns reading strategies that help with both learning to read and reading to learn.

REFLECTIVE BREAK

Before moving to Chapter 4, consider this reflection question:

- How does knowing about how ESOL students learn to read English help you in teaching reading?

4

What Are Reading Strategies?

The focus of this chapter is reading strategies.

REFLECTIVE BREAK

Before discussing reading strategies, it is important to distinguish between strategies and skills. Complete these two sentences:

- A strategy is _____.

- A skill is _____.

The difference between a strategy and a skill is automaticity. A skill is unconscious behavior, something people do without thinking. For example, a skilled tennis player reacts without thinking and hits the tennis ball with the racket. A strategy, on the other hand, is conscious behavior, something that a person thinks about before doing or acting. A young girl learning to play tennis has to think about what to do when playing. She may know she is supposed to hit the ball when it crosses over the net but has to think first, then react. She has strategies that have not yet become skills.

Relate this idea to reading strategies. Teachers cannot teach skills because they are unconscious behavior, so they must teach students strategies—conscious behavior—and give them opportunities to practice and use the strategies. Over time, with practice and use, the strategies may become skills.

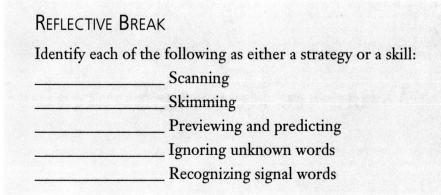

Identify each of the following as either a strategy or a skill:

_____ Scanning

_____ Skimming

_____ Previewing and predicting

_____ Ignoring unknown words

_____ Recognizing signal words

This is actually a trick activity! In fact, all of the preceding items might be either a strategy or a skill, depending on the individual. If used consciously, they are strategies; used unconsciously, they are skills. Which ones do you use, either as a strategy or a skill, in your reading, either L1 or L2?

Type	L1? L2?	
_____	_____	Scanning
_____	_____	Skimming
_____	_____	Previewing and predicting
_____	_____	Ignoring unknown words
_____	_____	Recognizing signal words

It may be difficult to know which reading skills you use because their use is unconscious. Reading a passage aloud may be helpful; this often brings a skill to the surface.

There are some critical points to know about teaching strategies. Research shows that

- Explaining why a strategy is important and when to use it helps students to learn it.

- It takes time. Students cannot be expected to learn a strategy a week.

- It requires practice and repetition. Students need to practice a strategy over and over.

- The more students practice a strategy in class, the more likely it is that they will use it outside of class. Encourage them to use the strategy on their own.

REFLECTIVE BREAK

- Have you taught reading strategies?

- If so, what happened? Did your students learn and use any of the strategies?

- What did you learn from reading this chapter?

Conclusion

This chapter focused on strategies and skills. Chapters 8 and 12 explore two types of reading strategies: fluency and comprehension.

With the foundation complete in Part I, Part II covers fluency, a critical aspect of reading that is generally overlooked or not understood by most reading teachers.

5

Reading Fluency

The goal of this chapter is to introduce the concept of fluency in ESOL reading instruction. By the end of this chapter, you will understand what reading fluency is.

What Is Reading Fluency?

> ### REFLECTIVE BREAK
>
> Think about fluency and reading; consider what fluent readers do. Now complete this sentence:
>
> - Reading fluency is _____.

When I ask ESOL teachers to complete this sentence, they usually write something about speed or reading fast. Although most reading experts do include some aspect of *rate* (that term is usually preferred to *speed*), speed reading is really not a crucial part of fluent reading. Rather, what these teachers may be thinking of is *automaticity*. Fluent reading involves *automaticity*, when something is done automatically: quickly, rapidly, and without thinking. A critical component of reading fluency involves the automatic recognition of words; fluent readers have efficient, effective word recognition skills that help them construct the meaning of a text.

There is more to automaticity than quickness or speed, however. As implied by these two words, *efficient* and *effective*, it also involves

←		→
Unknown Words	General Vocabulary	Sight Vocabulary

Figure 1. Knowledge Continuum for Reading Vocabulary

accuracy. When people read fluently, the automatic recognition of words is accurate and correct, every time. This automatic recognition of words involves *sight vocabulary*, words that readers know automatically (without thinking), correctly, every time, regardless of context. Sight vocabulary is part of reading vocabulary knowledge.

Reading vocabulary knowledge may be helpfully viewed as a continuum, shown in Figure 1. On one end of the continuum are words that readers do not know. In the middle of the continuum are words that are in their *general vocabulary*. These are words that, when readers come across them, require the reader to pause for a second or two to recall their meaning. At the other end of the continuum are words that are in the reader's sight vocabulary.

REFLECTIVE BREAK

Of particular importance is how words become part of sight vocabulary. Think about this statement and then answer this reflection question:

- How do words in people's general vocabulary become part of their sight vocabulary?

The best answer is *through reading.* When people read a good deal, they encounter words that are part of their general vocabulary. They pause briefly to recall their meaning and then continue reading. When readers come across the same words over and over again, these words gradually move along the continuum and become part of their sight vocabulary. The more people read, the larger their sight vocabulary becomes, and the larger their sight vocabulary becomes, the more fluent their reading becomes.

Now, to illustrate the important role that sight vocabulary plays in fluent reading, read these two sentences:

- The big dog ran after the small cat before I could stop it.
- Those covert forces employ both physical and psychological methods to intimidate its citizenry.

Each sentence has 13 words, but most likely you read each sentence slightly differently. You could probably read the first sentence quickly, but it took you somewhat longer to read the second one. The 13 words in the first sentence are in your sight vocabulary; however, several of the words in the second sentence are probably part of your general vocabulary.

So how does a fluent reader read? A fluent reader reads effortlessly and confidently at a level of understanding and a rate appropriate for the purpose or task and the material, seldom using a dictionary. This definition includes both the affective and cognitive dimensions of reading (see Chapter 1). The words *effortlessly* and *confidently* reflect the affective dimension. One way of thinking about *effortlessly* is to think of a river flowing smoothly. Now imagine readers' eyes flowing smoothly, effortlessly across the page as they read fluently. *Confidently* indicates that fluent readers know they can read; they do not hesitate. They read and expect to understand.

The cognitive dimension is found in the phrase, *a level of understanding . . . appropriate for the purpose or task and the material*. Fluent readers adjust their level of understanding of the materials they read; they do not read everything for 100% comprehension.

REFLECTIVE BREAK

Think about your own L1 reading:
- When do you read for 100% understanding?
- When do you read for less than 100% understanding?

The answers to the questions vary, of course. The important point is that readers do not always read for 100% understanding. Readers' reasons—their purposes or tasks—for reading a text are key factors in the level of understanding.

- What do you read for 100% understanding?
- What do you read for less than 100% understanding?

Now consider the rate at which readers read a text, and think about your own L1 reading:

- When do you read slowly and carefully?
- When do you read very fast?

Your answers most likely concern why you are reading the text (your purpose). Readers *scan* (read very quickly) a text when they are looking for specific information (e.g., the weather; the time of a movie); they *skim* (read quickly) when they want to get the overall or general meaning (e.g., to see if they want to check the book out of the library). They read *slowly* and *carefully* when they study a text for an examination.

The readability of a text also determines the rate. For instance, academic writing is often difficult to read not just because of the subject matter but because of the author's writing style. Also, technical or specialized vocabulary makes a text difficult to read.

Conclusion ⟍

This chapter covered reading fluency, a topic that, in my experience, most ESOL teachers know little, if anything, about. The next chapter discusses the role the fluency plays in reading.

REFLECTIVE BREAK

Before continuing on to Chapter 6, consider these reflection questions:

- What is the most important thing you have learned in this chapter?

- Why is it important?

6

Why Is Reading Fluency Important?

The previous chapter examined reading fluency. The aims of this chapter are to discuss the importance of fluency and explain why it should be a part of any English language reading program.

REFLECTIVE BREAK

In order to answer the question of why reading fluency is important, it is necessary to revisit the definition of reading given in Chapter 1. Can you recall it? Complete this sentence again:

• Reading is _____.

In case you cannot remember, here it is: *Reading is a number of interactive processes between the reader and the text, in which readers use their knowledge to build, to create, and to construct meaning.*

People's brains are powerful but limited in their capacity to hold and process new information. If, as a person reads, he must stop momentarily to understand the meaning of each word, or many words, in a sentence, the working memory becomes overloaded. When this happens, it is necessary to stop and read the sentence again, and if this happens with every sentence, the reader may have to go back to the beginning of the paragraph and read it again.

Further, if a reader does not quickly recognize and understand the syntax in the sentence she is reading, it may be necessary to stop to consider it. And, like a lack of word understanding, if this happens frequently, it may be necessary to go back to the beginning of the paragraph and read it again.

REFLECTIVE BREAK

- Is the following statement *true* or *false*?

_____ Fluency makes reading comprehension possible.

The correct answer is *true*. The research in both L1 and L2 reading is clear: Fluent readers are more efficient and effective readers than slow readers (Lightbown, Halter, White, & Horst, 2002; National Reading Panel, 2000). Slow readers cannot be fluent readers, and fluent readers understand more than slow readers.

In sum, reading fluency refers in part to efficient, effective word recognition skills and grammatical knowledge that help a reader to construct the meaning of a text. Fluency makes reading comprehension possible.

Unfortunately, most English language reading programs do not include reading fluency. Generally, the focus in such programs is comprehension: getting the meaning. As Part IV demonstrates, this involves comprehension questions and strategies. This is only part of the reading process, however; fluency makes comprehension possible.

Conclusion

Fluency plays a critical role in effective and efficient reading. Accordingly, the teaching of fluency has to be integrated into any ESOL reading program that has as a goal reading effectively and efficiently in English. How to teach fluency is the focus of Part III.

REFLECTIVE BREAK

Now that Part II is complete, consider these reflection questions:

- Has your understanding of reading changed?

- What do you think of fluency?

7

Extensive Reading

The goal of this chapter is to introduce extensive reading and demonstrate how it can be integrated into any ESOL reading program.

The best way to help students become fluent readers is by letting them read. People learn to read by reading: The more students read, the better readers they become. One approach to teaching ESOL reading that allows learners to practice reading a great deal is *extensive reading* (ER). The goals of ER are overall understanding as well as information and enjoyment. Good things happen when ESOL students read extensively. Studies show that they become fluent readers, learn many new words, and expand their understanding of words they knew before (Beglar, Hunt, & Kite, 2012). In addition, they write better (Hafiz & Tudor, 1989), and their listening and speaking abilities improve (Cho & Krashen, 1994). Perhaps the best result of ER found from numerous studies is that students develop positive attitudes toward reading and increased motivation to study English (Judge, 2011; Takase, 2007).

In ER, when students finish reading a book, they get another and read it. They do not answer comprehension questions or write book reports (which students often dislike writing and teachers often dislike reading), and they do not translate from English to their first language.

- What should students read, easy or hard books?

- Why?

If you answered *easy* for the first question, then you are correct. ER involves students reading many easy, interesting books. They must read books and other materials that are well within their *reading comfort zone*. When learners read books that are within their reading comfort zones, they are able to read for overall meaning easily; they do not need to worry about many difficult or unknown words. A quick strategy to help students determine whether a book is within their comfort zone is to have them open their books at random and read a page, counting the words that are not known. For beginning readers, more than one or two unknown words per page might make the book too difficult to read with general understanding. For intermediate learners, a text with no more than three or four unknown or difficult words per page usually is appropriate.

- True or false? Students choose what they want to read. Explain your answer.

The answer is *true, Learners choose what they want to read.* This is very important and related to the basis of ER: Readers learn to read by reading. Because students read material in which they are interested, they should be allowed to choose what (and where and when) to read. In ER, students also are free to stop reading books that they do not find interesting, or that are too hard or too easy.

When students are reading easy, interesting material that they select, their reading rate is usually faster, rather than slower. This helps develop fluency. Nuttall (1996) notes that "speed, enjoyment and comprehension are closely linked with one another" (p. 128). She describes "the vicious circle of the weak reader: Reads slowly; Doesn't enjoy reading; Doesn't read much; Doesn't understand; Reads slowly" and so on (p. 127). Extensive reading can help readers "enter instead the cycle of growth. . . . The virtuous circle of the good reader: Reads faster; Reads more; Understands better; Enjoys reading; Reads faster" (p. 127).

REFLECTIVE BREAK

- How much should students read in ER?
    a. It does not matter.
    b. They cannot read a lot because they are busy.
    c. They should read as much as possible.

The answer, of course, is *c. They should read as much as possible.* Teachers must make sure that their students are given the time and opportunity to read, read, and read some more because the more students read, the better readers they become. For beginning ESOL readers, the minimum is one book a week. Some ER teachers tell their students to read a certain number of words each week or read for a certain number of hours.

This leads to the topic of the reading material for ER. What should learners read? I advocate *language learner literature* (LLL), material that is specially written for language learners. The most common form of LLL is the *graded reader* (GR). GRs are written for specific grades or levels (e.g., beginners or level 1), using designated vocabulary and grammar. The vocabulary used in GRs is determined primarily by frequency of occurrence; for instance, the most frequent 75 or 100 words for a GR written at a basic level. Another characteristic of GRs is appropriate syntax: Beginning levels have simple syntax, and higher levels use more complex structures.

In addition to appropriate vocabulary and syntax, the *length* of GRs is controlled. The lower the grade, the shorter the GR. GRs written for beginners may be 10 to 15 pages with many illustrations to help convey meaning. GRs written for advanced learners may be 80 to 100 pages with few, if any, illustrations.

Complexity is also a feature of GRs. The plot of a GR novel written for beginners would not be as complex as a plot of a GR novel written for advanced learners. Moreover, there would not be as many characters in the beginning GR novel as the advanced novel.

ESOL teachers are fortunate because all of the major publishers offer GR series, which range from basic levels (e.g., 75 most frequent words) to advanced (e.g., 2,500 most frequent words).

One question that ESOL teachers may have about ER is, *How can I use ER in my own teaching, in my classroom?* ER can be integrated into any ESOL course or curriculum, without modifying goals and objectives. Here are four ways this can be done:

- Set up an ER course in which students read and do ER activities (see Bamford & Day, 2004).

- Add ER to an existing course. Most of the reading would be done outside of class; some class time would be used for reading and ER activities. Nothing is eliminated from the course. Instead, reading GRs is an additional requirement of the course. When you add ER to a course, it is important to give the students a grade for their reading. I use *reading targets:* Students have to read a certain number of books during the semester in order to get a certain grade. If the reading target is two books a week for a 10-week term, then the student would have to read 20 books to get full credit.

- Set up an after-school club. Students meet on a regular basis (e.g., every 2 weeks) to read books and do ER activities.

- Use homeroom period for ER. Students read GRs.

ER is the best way to help students become fluent readers, but there are two other ways: reading fluency strategies and reading fluency activities. The goal of fluency strategies and activities is to move learners from slow, laborious, ineffective word-for-word reading to fluent reading.

Conclusion

The goal of this chapter was to introduce extensive reading and show how it can be integrated into teaching ESOL reading to help students become fluent readers. Chapter 8 treats another approach to teaching fluency: fluency strategies.

REFLECTIVE BREAK

Before moving to Chapter 8, reflect on these questions:

- What do you think of extensive reading?

- Is it something you could integrate into your teaching?

- Why or why not?

8

Fluency Strategies

In addition to having students read extensively to gain fluency, teaching them reading fluency strategies is also beneficial. The aim of this chapter is to provide four fluency strategies:

- scanning
- previewing and predicting
- skimming
- ignoring unknown words

REFLECTIVE BREAK

- Do you recognize any of these strategies?
- Why do you think they are *fluency* strategies?

Scanning

Scanning is reading very quickly to find an answer to a question or find specific information. It is not slow reading to understand; rather, it is a rapid search for specific information.

Procedure

1. Introduce scanning. You might ask students how, what, and when they scan in their first language.

2. Using the text they have read, instruct your students to find a specific piece of information, such as a date, name, or phrase.

3. Give them a set period of time. You can encourage them to search quickly by announcing the amount of time remaining (e.g., "Ten seconds, five, four, three, two, one, stop!").

4. Have students practice scanning frequently.

5. Make sure each task is a bit more challenging than the previous one.

6. The more students practice this strategy in class, the more likely it is that they will use it outside of class. Encourage them to use scanning on their own.

Previewing and Predicting

Previewing and predicting is a useful strategy that helps readers get an introduction to a text. Research shows that readers read a text with greater understanding when they know something about it (Grabe, 2009, p. 47). I teach this strategy before teaching skimming because it prepares students for skimming.

Procedure

1. Before the students read a text, introduce previewing and predicting. Explain that *previewing* means looking at the text title and images (photos, drawings, graphs, etc.) *before* they start reading. After previewing, students should try to *predict* (make a guess about) the topic, what the text is about.

2. Tell them that using this strategy before reading can help them improve their understanding of the text when they read it.

3. Find an appropriate text with some illustrations. Make a multiple-choice question (e.g., three choices) about the topic of the text (e.g., *What do you think this article is about?*).

4. Give your students the text and the question about the topic. Instruct them to look quickly at the title and the illustrations and then answer the question.

5. Time them (e.g., 30 seconds).

6. Then have students read the text to check their answer.

Skimming

Skimming involves reading a text fast to get a general understanding of the topic. As mentioned previously, when readers know something about a text, their comprehension is better. This strategy gives a general idea of a book or an article, its content and organization.

Introduce skimming after students have practiced previewing and predicting. Previewing and predicting is an easy strategy for students to learn and serves as a good introduction to skimming.

Procedure

1. Before your students read a text, introduce skimming: reading very fast, without stopping to get the general meaning. Check to see if they skim in their first language. Explain that readers' understanding is better when they know about the topic.

2. To skim a book, tell your students to read rapidly:
   - the title and subtitle
   - the author(s)
   - the date of publication
   - the table of contents (What are the major sections and the titles of chapters?)
   - the introductions to the major sections
   - the first and concluding paragraphs of each chapter

3. To skim articles or chapters in a book, tell your students to read rapidly:
   - the title and subtitle
   - the author(s)
   - the abstract (if any)
   - the sections (both major and sub-)
   - the first sentence of each paragraph
   - any graphics (photos, maps, charts, etc.)
   - the final (or summary) paragraph

4. Have students practice the strategy.

5. Give students a set period of time depending on the reading they are going to skim. Encourage them to read quickly by announcing the amount of time remaining (e.g., "Two minutes . . . one minute . . . stop!"). It can be challenging to

know how much time to allow, so skim the text before class, timing yourself, and then use that time to calculate the time you will allow for your students to skim.

6. Consider giving the students a comprehension question about the general meaning of the text after they have skimmed it. For example, *The general meaning of the article is:* followed by three choices.

7. Have students practice skimming frequently.

8. Make sure each task is a bit more challenging than the previous one.

9. Encourage your students to use skimming on their own.

Ignoring Unknown Words

This useful fluency strategy of ignoring unknown words is relatively easy to teach and for students to learn. Readers use this strategy when reading in their L1. It simply involves ignoring unknown words and continuing reading.

Procedure

1. Find a reading that has several words your students do not know.

2. Compose several questions about the overall meaning of the text and the main ideas. Avoid questions that are concerned with supporting information or details.

3. Introduce the strategy. Tell your students that they do not need to know the meaning of every word to understand the meaning of a text.

4. Advise them to ignore words they do not know and to keep reading.

5. Now instruct them to read the text that you selected. Make sure they do not use their dictionaries. When they finish, they should answer the questions you prepared.

6. Have them read the text a second time to check their answers.

7. Finish by discussing how much they could understand without knowing all of the words.

Tips for Teaching Fluency Strategies

- Set a time limit (e.g., 30 seconds; 1 minute) for activities that you use to practice a fluency strategy. If a time limit is not given, students may simply read slowly and carefully to find the information.

- Do fluency strategy practice with readings that students have already read and that they understand. The focus is fluency, not understanding the reading.

Conclusion

This chapter presented four strategies that can help students become fluent readers. Bear in mind that fluency strategies need to be timed; otherwise, students might read slowly and carefully. In Chapter 9, the focus is fluency activities.

REFLECTIVE BREAK

- Do you think you could teach any of these fluency strategies?

- Why or why not?

9

Fluency Activities

This chapter looks at four activities to help learners develop reading fluency. An example accompanies each activity. You can easily make your own activities, using these examples as models. Similar to fluency strategy practice, fluency activities need to be timed.

Reading Faster

This fluency activity encourages students to try to read a text faster than they read it before. Do this three times with an article that is interesting and most can read.

Tell students:

1. Use a timer to time yourself.

2. Read the passage. How long did it take you? Write the time here: _____.

3. Now read the passage again to see if you can read it faster than the first time. How long did it take you? Write the time here: _____.

4. Read it a third time. Can you read it even faster? How long did it take you? Write the time here: _____.

Find the Same Word, Pair, or Phrase _____◣

In the chart below scan each line to find the phrase on the left. Phrases may appear more than once. Can you finish in 15 seconds? The first one is done for you.

	a	b	c	d	e
1. back out	back in	back up	back out	back side	back down
2. deal with	dealer	deal out	peal out	deal with	deal down
3. come up	come out	come up	come over	come in	come up
4. at odds	at odds	odds are	odds out	at odds	poor odds

Paced Reading _____◣

- Find an article on a topic that is of interest to your students and that the majority can read.

- Set a reading rate goal at which you would like your students to read. For example, if your students read slowly (fewer than 100 words per minute, or wpm) you could set the reading rate goal at 125 wpm. The purpose is to give a good idea of the rate at which they need to read in order to read 125 wpm.

- Divide the reading into four blocks of 125 words each.

- Distribute the reading and have your students read it. Time them for 4 minutes, announcing the time at 1-minute intervals.

- After each minute, regardless of where they are in the text, students go to the next block.

- If they finish reading a block before 1 minute is up, tell them to reread.

- Do this activity as often as possible. When you believe that the class is ready to move to a faster rate (e.g., 150 wpm), design a new reading.

- The number of reading blocks is up to you. You could have more or fewer, depending on the class time and the ability of your students.

Timed Repeated Reading

In this activity, learners read a familiar passage, generally one that they have previously read, for a certain amount of time, usually 1 to 3 minutes. Then they stop, go back to the beginning of the passage, and read again for the same amount of time. This procedure is then repeated. At the end of each timed period, when the teacher says *stop*, the students stop reading and underline the last word read. Instruct them to read at a comfortable rate, neither fast nor slow.

After the third reading, students count the number of words they read each time (wpm) and record them in a chart:

Name:			
Date	1st Reading #wpm	2nd Reading #wpm	3rd Reading #wpm

Conclusion

These four fluency activities, which students generally find enjoyable, can easily be adapted to fit your students' particular needs. Remember to time them. For more fluency activities, see Day (2012). Now that fluency and the teaching of fluency have been covered in Part II and Part III, continue on to Part IV, Comprehension.

> REFLECTIVE BREAK
>
> • Do any of these fluency activities appeal to you?
>
> • Why or why not?

What Is Comprehension?

This chapter is concerned with reading comprehension. It begins by examining comprehension and then explains six types of reading comprehension. After reading this chapter, you will have gained insights for teaching ESOL reading comprehension.

Reading Comprehension

> ### REFLECTIVE BREAK
>
> Complete this sentence:
>
> * Reading comprehension is _____.

Most likely your completed sentence includes words and phrases such as *getting the meaning, understanding,* and *decoding.* A more complete answer can be found by looking, once again, at the definition of reading given in Chapter 1. Can you recall it?

Reading is _____.

Just in case you forgot: *Reading is a number of interactive processes between the reader and the text, in which readers use their knowledge to build, to create, and to construct meaning.* This definition allows teachers to see comprehension as the product, or the result, of the interactive processes.

Your sentence probably has something to do with reading a text and answering *comprehension questions*. Using comprehension questions is common in ESOL reading courses and materials. This topic is covered in Chapter 11. Your sentence might also include *strategies*. The use of strategies to teach ESOL reading is the focus of most published materials. This topic is the focus of Chapter 12.

Viewing comprehension as a product means that it can be *measured*. Generally, reading comprehension is measured by comprehension questions, which take a variety of forms. Related to the measurement of comprehension is *accuracy*. The accuracy of an individual's understanding of a text can be measured as well. The focus of most ESOL reading instruction is comprehension; as mentioned in Chapter 5, fluency is often neglected, even though it is the basis of comprehension.

In sum, comprehension can be seen as

• the product, or result, of the interactive processes

• meaning, or understanding

• accuracy

• measurable (e.g., comprehension questions)

• the focus of most ESOL reading instruction

Types of Comprehension

In teaching comprehension, six types of comprehension are useful in helping students interact with their readings.

Literal Comprehension

REFLECTIVE BREAK

Complete this sentence:

- Literal comprehension is _____.

Literal comprehension is an understanding of the straightforward meaning of the text, such as facts. Literal comprehension questions can be answered directly from the reading. Check your students' literal comprehension first to make sure they have understood the basic meaning. An example of a literal comprehension question is: "What is literal comprehension?"

Reorganization

The second type of comprehension is *reorganization.* Students use information from various parts of the reading and combine them for additional understanding. For example, a reader might read at the beginning of a story that John Doe died in 2012; later, the reading might reveal that he was born in 1962. In order to answer the question, *How old was Mr. Doe when he died?*, the student has to combine information from different parts of the reading to get the correct answer. Questions that use this type of comprehension teach students to examine the text in its entirety.

Inference

Inference requires students to combine their literal understanding with their own knowledge. Students need to take information from the reading and relate it to what they know in order to make an inference.

REFLECTIVE BREAK

- Why might it be difficult for students to answer an inference question?

Students may find it difficult to answer inference questions because the information is not explicitly given in the reading. One way of helping them is to relate it to inferencing in the real world. For example, if your friend comes to class with a wet umbrella; you can infer that it is raining.

Prediction

Students use both their understanding of the story and their own knowledge of the topic to *predict* what might happen next or after a story ends. Consider using two types of prediction, while-reading and post-reading. To illustrate while-reading prediction: Students could read the first two paragraphs of a passage and answer a question about what might happen next.

Post-reading prediction questions, like while-reading questions, involve students by using information from the reading and their own knowledge. For example, consider a romance in which the woman and man are married at the end of the novel. A post-reading prediction question might be: *Do you think they will remain married? Why or why not?*

Making predictions *before* students read the text is a pre-reading fluency strategy, as discussed in Chapter 8.

Evaluation

Evaluation, the fifth type of comprehension, asks students to make a judgment about some aspect of the text. For example, an evaluation comprehension question about this chapter might be: *How will the information in this chapter be helpful to you in teaching reading?* When answering an evaluation question, readers must use both a literal understanding and their knowledge of the text's topic and related issues.

REFLECTIVE BREAK

- Why might ESOL students be reluctant to give an evaluation of a text?

Students might be hesitant to be critical of or disagree with the printed word due to cultural factors. Model possible answers to evaluation questions, and give both positive and negative aspects.

Personal Response

This type of comprehension, *personal response*, requires students to give answers that depend on their feelings for the text. The answers come from the students and not from the text. Although no personal responses are incorrect, students must relate to the content of the text and reflect a literal understanding of the material. For example, *What do you like or dislike about this chapter?*

Also, like evaluation questions, cultural factors may make some students hesitate to criticize. Modeling a variety of responses often helps to overcome this reluctance.

Conclusion

This chapter discussed comprehension, and following chapters will show how comprehension can be taught. Chapter 11 deals with comprehension questions; Chapter 12 with comprehension strategies.

REFLECTIVE BREAK

Before going to the next chapter, reflect on these two questions:

- Has your understanding of reading comprehension changed?

- What insights have you gained from this chapter?

11

Comprehension Questions

The purpose of this chapter is to present a picture of five forms of comprehension questions that can be used to teach the six types of comprehension described in Chapter 10. A second goal is to demonstrate that well-developed comprehension questions can help students begin to think critically and intelligently.

REFLECTIVE BREAK

- Have you used comprehension questions in your teaching?

- Did some work better than others?

Forms of Questions

Yes/No Questions

Yes/no questions can be answered with either *yes* or *no*. For example, *Is this book about teaching ESOL reading?*

REFLECTIVE BREAK

- What is the major drawback to using yes/no questions?

Although they are a common form of comprehension question, yes/no questions have the disadvantage of allowing the student a 50% chance of guessing the correct answer. Consider following up with other forms of questions to determine if the student has understood the text.

You can use yes/no questions to teach all six types of comprehension. When they are used with personal response or evaluation, consider following up with other question forms. For example, *Do you like teaching? Why?*

Alternative Questions

Alternative questions are two or more yes/no questions connected with *or*. For example, *Does this chapter discuss the use of questions to* teach *reading comprehension or to* test *reading comprehension?* You may want to follow up with other forms. Alternative questions work well with literal, reorganization, inference, and prediction types of comprehension.

True/False

Although true/false questions are often used in commercially published materials, be careful of relying exclusively on them. As with yes/no questions, students have a 50% chance of guessing the correct answer. Rather than simply accept a right answer, make sure to ask why the answer is correct.

True/false questions can be used to teach all six types of comprehension. Follow-up questions are helpful when used with personal response or evaluation: *True or false: I like this chapter. Why or why not?*

Wh- Questions

Questions beginning with *where, what, when, who, how,* and *why* are commonly called wh-questions. They help students gain a literal understanding of the text, with reorganizing information in the text, and making evaluations, personal responses, and predictions. You can also use them to follow up other question forms, such as yes/no and alternative. *How* and *why* help students go beyond a literal understanding.

Multiple Choice

Multiple-choice questions come from other question forms. For example,

When was this book published?

> *a. 2010*
>
> *b. 2011*
>
> *c. 2012*
>
> *d. 2013*

Often this question form has only one correct answer when dealing with literal comprehension.

The multiple-choice format makes wh- questions easier to answer than no-choice wh-questions because they give the students some possible answers. Students might be able to check the text to see if any of the choices are discussed, and then make a choice.

Multiple-choice questions are effective with literal comprehension. They can also be used with prediction and evaluation with follow-up questions or activities that allow students to explain their choices.

Three Important Considerations

Regardless of the type of comprehension or the question form, make sure that the questions are used to help students interact with the text. This can be done by making sure that students have the reading in front of them while answering questions. They should be able to refer to the reading because reading comprehension, not memory skills, is being taught.

Another consideration to ensure that the questions actually teach is avoiding *tricky questions*. Because the goal is helping students to improve their reading comprehension, resist the temptation to trick them with cleverly worded questions (e.g., a complex question in which one clause is true and the other is false). Negative wording in a question can also make it tricky. Such unclear or misleading questions tend to discourage students. It is better to ask about important aspects of the text with straightforward, unambiguous questions.

Finally, be aware that using comprehension questions in teaching reading can be overdone. Even highly motivated students can become bored answering 25 questions on a three-paragraph reading.

Conclusion

Well-designed comprehension questions can help students understand a text. Comprehension questions are only a means to an end, however; the use of questions by themselves does not necessarily result in readers who interact with a text utilizing the six types of comprehension presented in Chapter 10. To ensure that your students are actively involved in creating meaning, promote a discussion of the answers—both the right and wrong ones—through a combination of teacher-fronted and group activities. Also, comprehension strategies, the subject of Chapter 12, help learners interact with a text.

REFLECTIVE BREAK

To close this chapter, here is a true/false reflection question:

- True or false? By reading this chapter, I have gained a deeper understanding of comprehension questions.

- Explain your answer.

12

Comprehension Strategies

Having students answer questions is one means to learn to read. Teaching learning comprehension strategies is also beneficial. The aim of this chapter is to provide five comprehension strategies:

- reread the story
- use your knowledge of the topic to help you read
- find main ideas in paragraphs
- recognize supporting information
- distinguish between fact and opinion

REFLECTIVE BREAK

- Do you recognize any of these strategies?
- Why do you think they are comprehension strategies?

Reread the Story

When a reader reads a text a second time, she understands it better. Research has demonstrated clearly that the more a person knows about a reading (e.g., topic, organization), the greater her comprehension is. So when students read a text a second time, obviously their comprehension increases. This strategy is simple but effective.

Procedure

1. First read the story.

2. Do not stop for words you do not know.

3. Then read it a second time.

Use Your Knowledge of the Topic to Help You Read

Remind students that understanding is an interaction between the reader and the text. Good readers use their knowledge of the topic to help them read a text. This easy-to-use strategy helps students achieve greater comprehension.

Procedure

1. First, use the previewing and predicting fluency strategy (see Chapter 8).

2. Next, think about what you know about the topic of the reading.

3. Then think about what information you might find in the reading.

4. Now read the story.

Find Main Ideas in Paragraphs

Finding main ideas in paragraphs is an important strategy in reading academic texts. Generally, every paragraph has a main idea, the most important information the writer wants to convey. The main idea is often near the beginning of the paragraph.

Procedure

1. Look for *cover* ideas (i.e., ideas that include other ideas).

2. Become familiar with the places where academic authors typically state their main ideas, and check those places within the text.

3. Look at subheadings to see if they suggest main ideas.

4. Watch for paraphrases and repetition; these often signal points authors feel are worth repeating.

5. Read the abstract or introduction, and the summary (if there is one) to find the main ideas stated or restated.

You can use a number of activities to teach this strategy. The following activity is particularly helpful.

Activity

1. Find a reading that has a main idea in each paragraph. You might have to revise the paragraphs to make sure each one has an identifiable main idea. Number the paragraphs.

2. On a piece of paper, write each main idea, but not in the order in which they appear in the reading. Photocopy it and give it to the students.

3. Instruct your students to read the text, using some of the procedures listed above to find the main idea in each paragraph.

4. When they finish reading the text, have them write the paragraph number next to its main idea.

Recognize Supporting Information

The ideas and facts that authors use to prove or explain their main ideas and the structures they use to present this information are called *supporting information*. It supports or reinforces the main idea of a paragraph.

In academic reading, students need to be able to recognize and evaluate how sound a claim is. In order to do this, they must be able to find the main ideas and then the supporting evidence.

Procedure

1. Give students examples of common types of supporting information, such as
   * examples
   * facts or statistics
   * reasons
   * cause-and-effect

- compare–contrast
- classification
- descriptions
- steps or procedures (time sequence/process/chronological)

2. Find a reading with good uses of supporting information.

3. Prepare a matching activity with supporting information in Column A and the main ideas they support in Column B. For example,

Column A: Supporting Information	Column B: Main Ideas
____ 1. astronauts	a. to show an old drug being used in a new way
____ 2. Maria Koike	b. to show an old drug being used in a traditional way
____ 3. people with high blood pressure	c. to show a situation that future drugs might treat

4. Distribute the reading and the handout.

5. Instruct your students to scan the text for the supporting information in Column A and match them with the main ideas they support in Column B.

Distinguish Between Fact and Opinion

It is important to know the difference between a *fact* and an *opinion*. A fact is something that happened or is true. An opinion is someone's idea or belief; it can also be an expression of agreement or disagreement.

Procedure

1. Use a reading with facts and opinions.

2. Make an activity with a number of statements.

3. Instruct your students to read the text and then identify the statements as either facts or opinions.

REFLECTIVE BREAK

Reflect on your own teaching:

- Do you use any of these comprehension strategies?

- If you do, which ones?

- Are they helpful?

Conclusion

If your students learn and use these five comprehension strategies, their reading comprehension will improve. Of course, there are many more comprehension strategies and activities you can use in your classroom (see Day, 2012).

REFLECTIVE BREAK

- What was the most helpful thing you learned in this chapter?

- How might it be helpful?

13

Planning the Reading Lesson

The purpose of this chapter is to look at how to plan a reading lesson. By the end of this chapter, you will be able to plan effective reading lessons.

REFLECTIVE BREAK

- A lesson plan is _____.

Although there is no single definition, a lesson plan can be viewed as *a teacher's description of what he or she will do in teaching a class.* Such descriptions may take at least two forms. They may exist only in the teacher's mind—with no hard copies—or a in a written lesson plan.

REFLECTIVE BREAK

- What form is your typical lesson plan? Written? In your head?

- Why?

The informational content of lesson plans also varies. They may contain detailed information, including learning outcomes (LOs), activities, materials, notes, instructions for students, homework assignments, assessment tasks, and timelines. Other plans may be simply an outline of what the teacher would like to do in the class.

Some teachers, particularly experienced ones, use lessons plans as a guide or a road map. They often deviate from what they have planned, depending on a number of factors, such as something that came up in class that they had not anticipated, a difficulty in a planned activity, or the atmosphere in the class (e.g., students were bored or uninterested). Teachers with little experience tend to continue using their lesson plans regardless of the success of the plan.

A number of elements are helpful in planning to teach a reading class. These elements often include LOs, activities to achieve the LOs, materials needed (e.g., readings, handouts), and homework assignments. The first step is to determine what you want your students to learn: the LOs. LOs are critical to planning an effective reading lesson because teachers need to know what they want their students to learn—to be able to do—by the end of the lesson.

Some LOs for an extensive reading lesson are

• select books to read that are within the students' reading comfort zones

• think creatively through writing about their books in ways that encourage original and expressive ideas

• engage in creative thinking and writing about the books they have read

• be able to recognize the plot and characters in a story

Some LOs for fluency are

- increase students' skimming rate
- increase their scanning rate
- ignore unknown words

Some LOs for comprehension are

- make inferences
- answer a personal response question
- identify main ideas in paragraphs

Once a teacher has developed the LOs, it is necessary to design activities or tasks to achieve them. It is important to make a specific connection between the activities and the LOs, that is, there should be at least one activity or task for each LO.

REFLECTIVE BREAK

- **Make some activities for one of the LOs above.**

Farrell (2009) offers seven useful principles when developing lesson plans for a reading class (pp. 74–78). These are particularly helpful:

1. Use reading materials that are interesting.
2. Make reading the major activity of the reading lesson.
3. Have a specific objective for each lesson.
4. Choose appropriate reading materials.

Additionally, consider these three principles:

1. Think about how you will know if you have achieved your LOs.
2. Consider what could go wrong and what you would do if that happened.
3. Reflect after the lesson. What happened?

Conclusion

An effective reading lesson plan can take many forms and involve a variety of different elements. There is no one approach to an effective reading lesson given the diversity of teachers, students, and contexts.

> ### REFLECTIVE BREAK
>
> • What factors do you find most important in planning an ESOL reading lesson?

14

Conclusion

The overarching goal of this book is to engage teachers in reflection on how reading may be taught to ESOL learners.

As a final activity, return to Chapter 2, and complete the question-naire again. Try not to look at your original responses. When you are finished, complete the final Reflective Break.

REFLECTIVE BREAK

- Were any of your ideas about ESOL teaching and learning confirmed?

- Did you learn something new?

- Did you change your mind about some aspect of ESOL reading?

References

Bamford, J., & Day, R. R. (Eds.). (2004). *Extensive reading activities for teaching language*. Cambridge, England: Cambridge University Press.

Beglar, D., Hunt, A., & Kite, Y. (2012). The effect of pleasure reading on Japanese university EFL learners' reading rates. *Language Learning, 62*(3), 1–39.

Cho, K., & Krashen, S. D. (1994). Acquisition of vocabulary from the Sweet Valley Kids series: Adult ESL acquisition. *Journal of Reading, 37,* 662–667.

Day, R. R. (Ed.). (2012). *New ways in teaching reading, revised*. Alexandria, VA: TESOL International Association.

Farrell, T. S. C. (2009). *Teaching reading to English language learners*. Thousand Oaks, CA: Corwin Press.

Grabe, W. (1991). Current developments in second language reading research. *TESOL Quarterly, 25*(3), 375–397.

Grabe, W. (2009). *Reading in a second language: Moving from theory to practice*. Cambridge, England: Cambridge University Press.

Hafiz, F., & Tudor, I. (1989). Extensive reading and the development of language skills. *ELT Journal, 43*(1), 4–13.

Judge, P. (2011). Driven to read: A multiple case study of enthusiastic readers in an extensive reading program at a Japanese high school. *Reading in a Foreign Language, 23,* 161–186.

Lightbown, P., Halter, R., White, J., & Horst, M. (2002). Comprehension-based learning: The limits of "Do it yourself." *Canadian Modern Language Review, 58,* 427–464.

National Reading Panel. (2000). *Teaching children to read: An evidence-based assessment of the scientific research literature on reading and its implications for reading instruction.* Washington, DC: National Institutes of Child Health and Human Development.

Nuttall, C. (1996). *Teaching reading skills in a foreign language* (2nd ed.). Oxford, England: Heinemann.

Takase, A. (2007). Japanese high school students' motivation for extensive L2 reading. *Reading in a Foreign Language, 19*, 1–19.

Suggested Readings and Sources

Day, R. R., et al. (2011). *Bringing extensive reading into the classroom.* Oxford, England: Oxford University Press.

This easy-to-read book guides teachers through the different ways of using extensive reading through four case studies describing projects in a range of learning environments.

Day, R. R., & Bamford, J. (1998). *Extensive reading in the second language classroom.* Cambridge, England: Cambridge University Press.

This comprehensive examination of extensive reading shows how reading large quantities of language learner literature helps students learn to read and develop positive attitudes and increased motivation to read. It has a wealth of practical advice for implementing extensive reading in the classroom.

The Extensive Reading Foundation. www.erfoundation.org.

The Extensive Reading Foundation is a not-for-profit, charitable organization whose initiatives include the annual Language Learner Literature Award for the best new works in English, maintenance of a bibliography of research on extensive reading, helping educational institutions set up extensive reading programs through grants that fund books and other reading material, and an online *Guide to Extensive Reading*, a highly recommended, free publication.

Reading in a Foreign Language. (nflrc.hawaii.edu/rfl)

This free, online, scholarly journal has a number of useful articles on extensive reading and reading fluency.

Also Available in the English Language Teacher Development Series

Reflective Teaching (Thomas S. C. Farrell)

Teaching Listening (Ekaterina Nemtchinova)

Teaching Pronunciation (John Murphy)

Language Classroom Assessment (Liying Cheng)

Cooperative Learning and Teaching (George Jacobs & Harumi Kimura)

Classroom Research for Language Teachers (Tim Stewart)

Teaching Digital Literacies (Joel Bloch)

Teaching Reading (Richard Day)

Teaching Grammar (William Crawford)

Teaching Vocabulary (Michael Lessard-Clouston)

Teaching Writing (Zuzana Tomas, Ilka Kostka, & Jennifer A. Mott-Smith)

English Language Teachers as Administrators (Dan Tannacito)

Content-Based Instruction (Margo Dellicarpini & Orlando Alonso)

Teaching English as an International Language
(Ali Fuad Selvi & Bedrettin Yazan)

Teaching Speaking (Tasha Bleistein, Melissa K. Smith, & Marilyn Lewis)

www.tesol.org/bookstore
tesolpubs@brightkey.net
Request a copy for review
Request a Distributor Policy